TORFAEN LIBRARIES
WITHDRAWN

Book No. 70026117

WHY AI?

All your questions about AI answered by a computer scientist

DR DHARINI BALASUBRAMANIAM

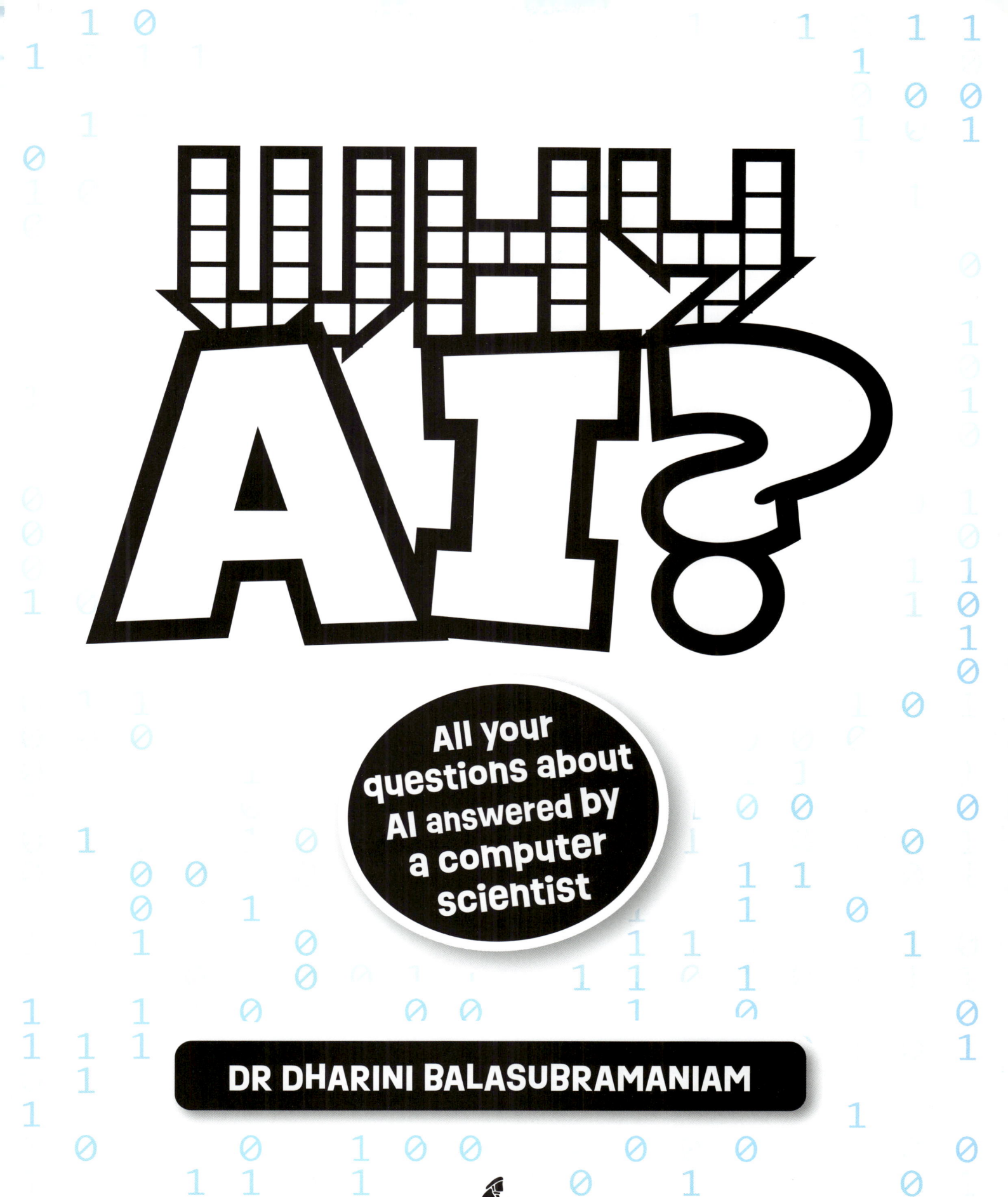

WAYLAND

First published in Great Britain in 2024 by Wayland

Text © Dharini Balasubramaniam 2024

Design © Hodder & Stoughton 2024

All rights reserved.

Commissioning Editor: Grace Glendinning
Designer: Arvind Shah

ISBN: 978 1 5263 2787 1 HBK
ISBN: 978 1 5263 2788 8 PBK
ISBN: 978 1 5263 2789 5 EBOOK

Printed and bound in China.

Wayland, an imprint of
Hachette Children's Group
Part of Hodder & Stoughton
Carmelite House
50 Victoria Embankment
London EC4Y 0DZ

An Hachette UK Company
www.hachette.co.uk
www.hachettechildrens.co.uk

Photo credits:
Alamy: Steve Bloom Images 4bl; Dpa picture alliance 9bl; GL Archive 6t; Pictorial Press Ltd 8t; The Canadian Press 9tl.
Stanford University: 8cl;
Shutterstock: Abscent Vector 14t; agsandrew/elements courtesy of NASA 16t; Aha-Soft 13b; Alina.Alina 17t; AlinStock 39b; all_is_magic 29b; ArtHead 10tr; Aslysun 45br; Arthur Balitskii 11crb; Dominik Ball 28-29t, 28b; BestforBest 33cr; Ihor Biliavskyi 6c, 9bc, 11c; BreezyVector 15b; Roman Chazov 11bl; Christakova 42c; Jamie Christoforou 25cr; cosmic_pony 21br; Denvitruk f cover c,7c,18b; Jamie Depledge 3bg,7t; Elenabsl 3b,6b, 16br, 31br; Juan Gaertner 35c; Maxim Gaigul 45tr; GoodStudio 26-27b; Golden Sikora 18c, 19c; Gorodenkoff f cover 1tr, 18t, 22c, 45cl; Graphic farm 33cl;graficriver_icons_logo f cover br, 11tcr; Kaspars Grinvalds 21bl;Ground Picture 44bl, 45bl; Gussno Creative 32cr; Iconic Bestiary 10bc, 11clb;Illustrator 096 40bl; Imagin Studio 45bc; Nicoleta Ionescu 7cr; Leo Iv 41b; Ivector 14b; Jamesbin 8-9bg; Puwadol Jaturawuttichai 38c;Ilya Kalinin 20c; Dimitrios Karamitros 30b; Kiantee 23tr; Igor kisselev 11tc; Klyaksun 12; Aliaksei kruhlenia 8b; Raroslav Kryuchka 44c; Igor Kyrlytsya 22-23; Ilya Lukichev 16bl;Macrovector 4t; Magic pictures 24-24bg, 25t; males_design 4br, 5r; Martial Red 24bl, 27cl; Marish 5cr; Masterandi 24c; Maxuser 11cr; ME Image 38b; Mentalmind 40t; Metamorworks 31tl, 35t; Mhatzapa 41t; Konstantin Mirinov 25cl;Ded Mityay 13c; Nadya_Art 42l, 43r; Net Vector 39c; Notion Pic 37t; Aexander_P 11tr; Yauhen Paleski 7ccl;peopleimages.com Yuri A 10tc, 23c; Phonlamai Photo 36b,37b,44cl; theodore Popov 21t;Pranch 24br;Proffiphoto f cover bl; ProStockStudio 3t,13t,43b; PST Vector 21bc; nastitsa Ptitsa 32-33bg;Hamzar_Qamar 10bl;Heena Rajpu 25b; RedlineVecto 7cl; Remo_Designer 8bc; Robuart 14c; R-Type 45t; Round Squid 19b; Sammby 29c; Es Sarawuth 19r; Scharfsinn 31cr; Hryshchyshen Serhiii 27tr; Olexander Simkina f cover cl, 6ccl; Shmai 6cr; SK Imagine 45tl; Song_about_summer 17b; Stock-Asso 22b, 45cr; Stokkete f cover 1tl; Irina Streinikova 40br; Suwin 28c, 29c;Tatik22 6cl; Paisit Teerapharsakool 11br; The Studio 21tr; Thinkhubstudio 33b;TippaPatt 26c; Topvector 21c; Triff 11cl; Josiah True 43t; Vasabii 10bcl, 21cl; Vector Image Plus 41r; VectorPot 28t; Vegorus f cover bg, 1bg; Vershinin89 44cr; ViJul f cover c inset; Pavel Vinnik 30-31; Vitaforyat 11bc; Vs148 28-29bg;Woocat 34b, 35b;Konstantin Yuganov 44br.
Wikimedia: Cynthia Breazeal 9tr CCA-SA; Bengt Oberger 9tc CCA-SA.

CONTENTS

What is AI? 4–5
When did AI start? 6–7
Who are the pioneers of AI? 8–9
Why do we need AI? 10–11
What can AI do? 12–13
How does AI work? 14–15
Where can we use AI? 16–19
Search: AI problem-solving 20–21
Example 1: game engines 22–23
Natural language processing 24–25
Example 2: smart assistants 26–27
Robotics 28–29
Example 3: autonomous cars 30–31
Machine learning 32–33
Example 4: generative AI 34–35
What should AI do? The rights and wrongs 36–37
What is the future of AI? 38–39
What other subjects are useful for AI? 40–41
What if? 42–43
How would you like to use AI? 44–45
Glossary 46
Further information 47
Index 48

What is AI?

To understand AI, we first need to understand what it is and how it got its name: **artificial intelligence**. Let's begin with the most basic question.

What is intelligence?

Intelligence is the ability to gain knowledge and skills, and to use them in a logical and sensible way. Something that is intelligent can apply its knowledge and skills to make correct decisions in new situations.

Who or what can have intelligence?

When we use the word intelligent to describe different kinds of things, we can break down the definition even more:

Natural intelligence in humans and other animals

Artificial intelligence in machines, such as computers

So, how does artificial intelligence come about?

One of the founders of the idea of artificial intelligence, John McCarthy (see page 8), said it simply:

> [AI] is the science and engineering of making intelligent machines, especially intelligent computer programs.

Another way to think about AI is as the ability of computer programs to *imitate* the way humans make decisions and solve problems. Humans can use the information available to us logically, and make intelligent decisions. If we can program machines to do the same, we create artificial intelligence.

Humans are complicated

A rational person will make sensible decisions based on what they know. But humans don't always behave in a rational way. So, AI can be made:

- to try and copy humans in all their complex ways of viewing the world, or
- to always be logical and rational.

Types of AI

- **NARROW (also called weak) AI** can solve specific problems. This is the type of AI in use now.

- **STRONG AI** can solve general problems and plan for the future in a way similar to, or better than, humans. This type of AI has not yet been made, although some researchers think that the latest generative AI chatbots (see pages 32–35) are a step in this direction.

When did AI start?

In 1950, British mathematician Alan Turing asked the question:

Can machines think?

This essentially started the conversation around AI, which continues today.

TIMELINE: AI THROUGH THE DECADES

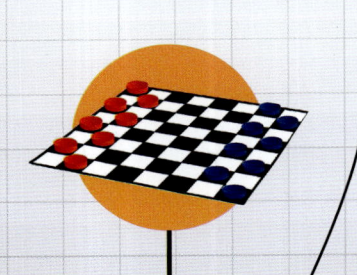

1950s
> The Turing Test (see page 8) for machine intelligence was proposed.

> The term Artificial Intelligence was introduced.

> The first ever running AI program (called Logic Theorist) was made.

> AI that could play games was introduced for playing draughts (checkers) and chess.

> The term 'machine learning' was introduced.

1960s
> ELIZA, a natural language processing program (see pages 24–25) that could 'chat' through written text, was created.

> Work on the first expert systems began (see page 15).

> Breakthroughs were made on machine learning models called neural networks (see page 15).

1970s
> The world's first 'intelligent' robot was created.

1980s
> The first self-driving car was built.

> Neural networks that could train themselves became more popular.

> Expert systems began to be used more widely in computer programming.

Developments

The early research and thinking around AI could be done by individuals or small groups.

But advances in AI needed a lot of resources, such as powerful computers. So, a lot of the later progress in AI was made in institutions or tech companies, which had access to these resources.

2000s

> More advanced self-driving vehicles were demonstrated on roads.

> Robots began to be used regularly in the home and to explore in harsh conditions in space and under the sea.

> Large amounts of data became available for training AI programs.

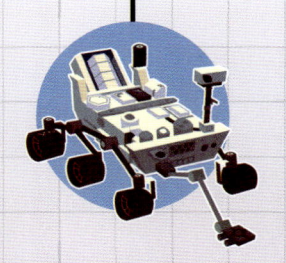

2020s

> Work on generative AI advances in speed and complexity.

> AI programs capable of generating different kinds of original content, such as artwork and stories, are released for use by the public.

1990s

> Chess program Deep Blue beat the chess world champion and grandmaster, Gary Kasparov.

> The first speech recognition software (AI understanding human language) was produced.

> The first artificially intelligent pets were created.

2010s

> Computer hardware became much more advanced – AI programs could run faster.

> The IBM Watson computer beat two past champions to win the US trivia game show *Jeopardy!*

> AI-based smartphone apps (such as, Siri and Cortana) were able to answer questions and offer suggestions in natural languages, such as English.

> The AlphaGO program beat the European and world champions in the game Go.

> Work on generative AI, which can create new content, began (see pages 34–35).

Who are the pioneers of AI?

Many researchers in different subjects have contributed to the development of AI. Here we look at some of them.

Alan Turing is thought of as the 'Father of Computer Science'. He is widely known for his work on code breaking during the Second World War (1939–45). But he was also interested in the idea that, like humans, machines could learn.

He proposed a test for machine intelligence, called the Turing Test (also called the Imitation Game):

- One machine (A) and one human (B) are asked questions by another human (C). All are in separate rooms and can interact only by typing.
- A tries to make C think that A is human. B tries to help C make the right decision.
- If C can't decide which of the others is the machine and which is the human, the machine passes the intelligence test!

John McCarthy was considered another 'Father of AI'. He first proposed the term Artificial Intelligence.

McCarthy also defined the programming language Lisp, used in many areas of AI, including robotics. He also worked on an early self-driving vehicle and on ways to make programs imitate how humans make decisions.

Arthur Samuel was the first person to use the term 'machine learning'. He also wrote the first self-learning program using machine learning techniques. This program learned to play draughts (checkers). In 1961, it beat a human champion.

Samuel also worked on speech recognition by machines, which is now used by smart assistants every day.

Geoffrey Hinton is known as one of the 'Godfathers of Deep Learning'. Work done by him and his colleagues has led to advances in computer vision (see page 29), image and speech recognition and natural language processing (see pages 24–25).

Hinton has also spoken out against the dangers of uncontrolled development of AI.

Barbara J. Grosz developed some of the early computer dialogue systems that could have conversations with humans. She also pioneered ideas of how different AI can work and communicate together.

Grosz has also worked to make sure university computer science programmes include discussing the ethics (rights and wrongs) of AI.

Cynthia Breazeal is a pioneer in social robotics, human–robot interaction and AI education. She led the development of Kismet, a robot that uses facial expressions, head positions and different tones of voice to communicate. Breazeal used child psychology to help Kismet learn from its interactions, and cartoon animators to make it more lifelike.

Joy Buolamwini is called a 'poet of code'. She uses art to point out the effects of AI on society, including the risks of trusting AI to be always right and the need for careful testing for all user groups. For example, many early AI facial recognition programs did not work correctly with people from different ethnic groups.

Buolamwini started the Algorithmic Justice League with the aim of holding technology responsible for the results of its use.

Mustafa Suleyman co-founded multiple AI companies, including DeepMind Technologies, which created AI programs capable of learning to play video and strategy games. He has also worked on applying AI to solve problems in the fields of energy and health and has spoken on the need for ethical AI.

I'm here to help!

Why do we need AI?

So, WHY AI? What value does it have and why is it being used more and more every day?

Human limits

AI means programming machines in the ways humans think and make decisions, and even improving on them.

Most people agree that humans are better at certain types of task, for example, those that need imagination, long-term plans or common sense. But humans are usually not so good at dealing with large amounts of data, and fast.

Modern machines for modern times

Humans and their devices now produce lots of useful data – while working, studying, shopping, playing games and travelling. But human brains find it difficult to process this amount of data and spot connections.

To process data with traditional computer software, its human programmers need to know exactly how to solve problems using the set of data, or how to pull information from it. They would then write programs to do this. AI is built to analyse data itself.

HUMAN DATA OVERLOAD

A helping hand

AI can quickly process large amounts of data. It helps humans by finding useful details and making new discoveries, without the need for specific programming for each task. It can even predict future events, such as changes in the weather.

By making sense of data, AI can help humans make better decisions and solve complex problems.

AI can improve our lives by doing the work we may find boring, helping scientists find better medicines, letting us talk directly to our devices, and making gaming more interesting.

11

What can AI do?

Some AI topics are more well-known that others. For example, we hear a lot about robots and chatbots. But AI can do much more!

Discovery

AI can discover new knowledge from existing data, even if:

- we didn't collect the data for this **particular knowledge**
- we don't already have the **rules** to find the knowledge from that data.

This means that data we have can be analysed by AI for new information and in ways we haven't thought about.

Aha!

Predictions and recommendations

AI can predict what might happen *in the future* and *recommend* things of interest to us based on existing data.

This kind of AI is already used a lot, for example, when you go online and a favourite website suggests an interesting video or product for you (*see page 17* for more on how companies use this).

Problem-solving

AI can solve problems and answer questions for users based on data, without specific instructions on how.

Recognising visual information

AI can look at images and other visual input and recognise shapes, patterns, people and objects.

Recognising language

AI can recognise 'natural language' – written or spoken – and either act on the words (the input) or translate them into another form.

Decision-making

AI can select the best option among many, based on the data available, and can rank options according to the user's needs.

How does AI work?

Like most computer programs, AI uses algorithms and data to produce its results.

What's an algorithm?

An algorithm is a set of instructions. These instructions are done in a particular order to complete a task or solve a problem. The original data to be processed by the algorithm is called the **input**. The result of the process is called the **output**.

Purpose of programs

Many computer programs are written to automate (reduce the need for human involvement in) the work humans do. For example, a program may search out fares for a flight from different airlines and list them according to price, or a program could turn on the heating if a room gets too cold.

AI takes it further

AI is also used to automate tasks that humans find difficult or ones that will take humans an extremely long time to do.

So **how** does AI do it?

AI techniques can be largely divided into **symbolic AI** and **connectionist AI**.

Symbolic AI

Symbolic AI – also called classic AI – works by capturing **existing real-world knowledge** and applying **rules** to it to solve problems.

With symbolic AI methods, AI's ability to learn new things is limited, but we can be more confident that the results are correct.

Symbolic AI methods can include:

1. Constraint solvers
These can solve problems such as Sudoku puzzles.

2. Expert systems
These use stored knowledge and rules to make decisions or recommendations for a situation.

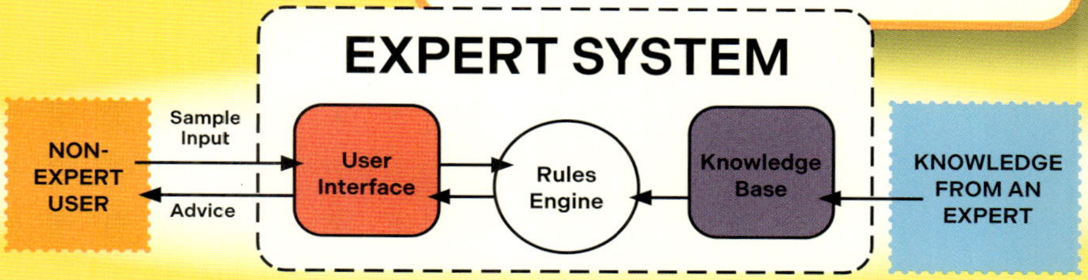

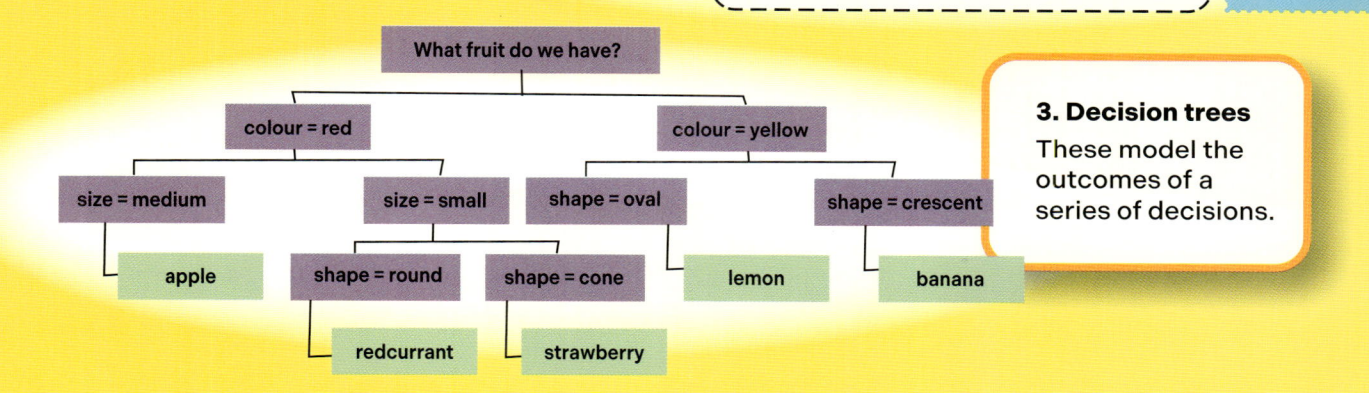

EXPERT SYSTEM

NON-EXPERT USER → Sample Input → User Interface ↔ Rules Engine ↔ Knowledge Base ← KNOWLEDGE FROM AN EXPERT
User Interface → Advice → Non-Expert User

3. Decision trees
These model the outcomes of a series of decisions.

What fruit do we have?
- colour = red
  - size = medium → apple
  - size = small
    - shape = round → redcurrant
    - shape = cone → strawberry
- colour = yellow
  - shape = oval → lemon
  - shape = crescent → banana

Connectionist AI

Connectionist AI works **without rules.** It learns patterns and relationships just from data. The more data, the better. It does not need much prior knowledge.

This technique can learn a lot more than symbolic AI from the data we give it, but needs huge amounts of data to work. We can't always be sure **what** it has learned or that what it learns is **sensible**.

Connectionist AI includes:

Artificial neural networks
These are used for machine learning (*see more on pages 32–33*). The hidden layers of a neural network are where the learning and pattern-making happens, using a complex set of mathematical processes.

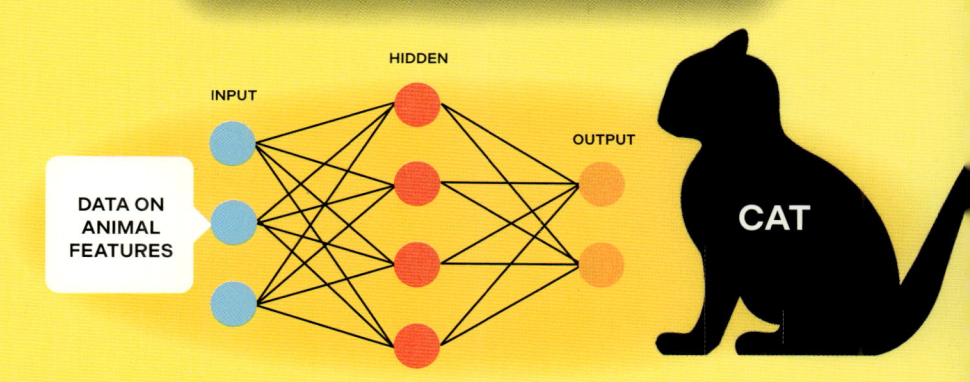

DATA ON ANIMAL FEATURES → INPUT → HIDDEN → OUTPUT → CAT

Where can we use AI?

AI can be used for so many different purposes. From science to shopping, AI's capabilities come in very handy for humans.

Scientific discoveries

Scientists collect lots of data for their research. AI can be used to look at this complex set of data and find new information.

For example, in astronomy, AI is used to find planets in other solar systems, or other galaxies and stars based on a huge set of data from telescopes.

Healthcare

If information about our health is available digitally (meaning, it can be read and processed by a computer), we can use AI to:

- make more accurate diagnoses of illnesses
- create new medicines and vaccines that can better treat illnesses
- support tasks such as scheduling appointments and digitising medical notes
- carry out machine-led surgeries.

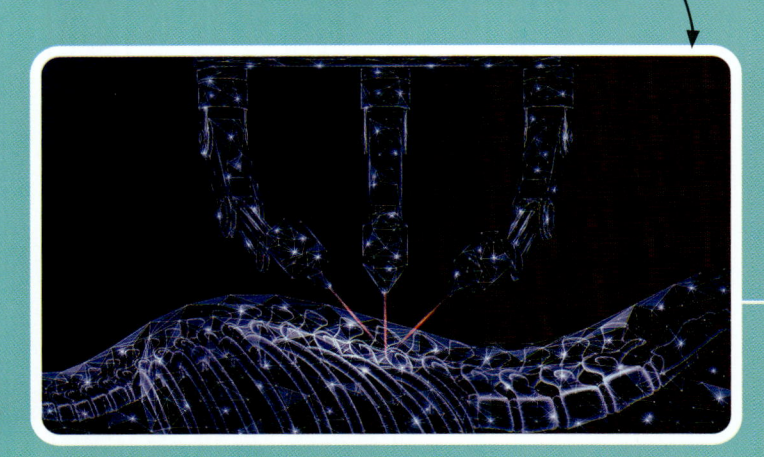

Shopping

Shops can keep data on what their customers buy, and use AI programs to guess what customers **might buy in future** and to **suggest new items** that could be interesting to them.

Online shops also have AI shopping assistants and chatbots that can help customers **find and choose what they need**, which is essentially AI-personal shopping.

Saving time, spending money!

Entertainment

Content creators and games developers can use AI to analyse user behaviour. Then creators can focus on **making more of what users want**, and recommending content specific to their interests.

AI can also analyse content (such as text, images, audio and video) to get useful **insights on trends and opinions** among users, while they play the games and as they go about their day.

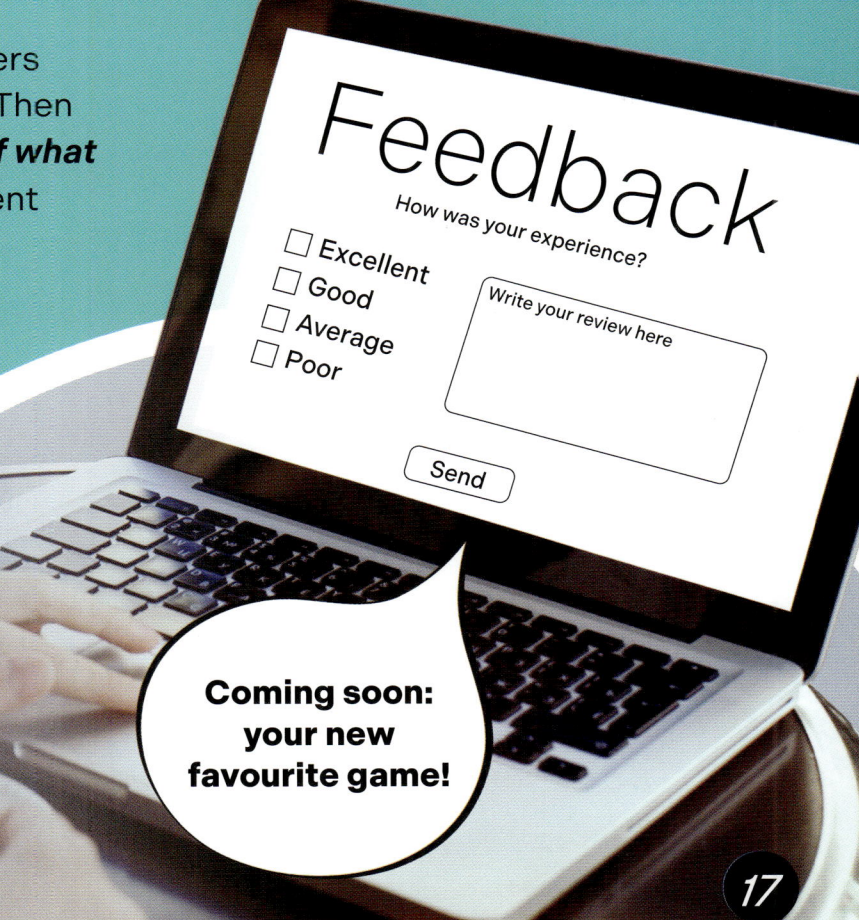

Coming soon: your new favourite game!

Manufacturing and logistics

Companies such as factories and transport businesses can use AI to:

- predict customer demand so they can make the right amount of a product at the right time
- improve the usefulness and efficiency of their machines and processes, reducing wasted materials, time and effort
- check the quality of services and goods before they are sold to users.

Agriculture

'Precision agriculture' is where farmers use AI to decide which crops should be planted where and when. AI can also help spot problems with soil and plants before the issues spread or do a lot of damage.

Education

- AI can be used to sort out complicated timetables to avoid clashes for pupils, and so that staff can focus on teaching.
- Some types of schoolwork can be automatically marked by AI programs.
- AI bots can answer routine questions, saving time for both teachers and pupils.
- Schools and universities can develop personalised learning programmes by analysing student data and adapting the programmes to suit students' needs.

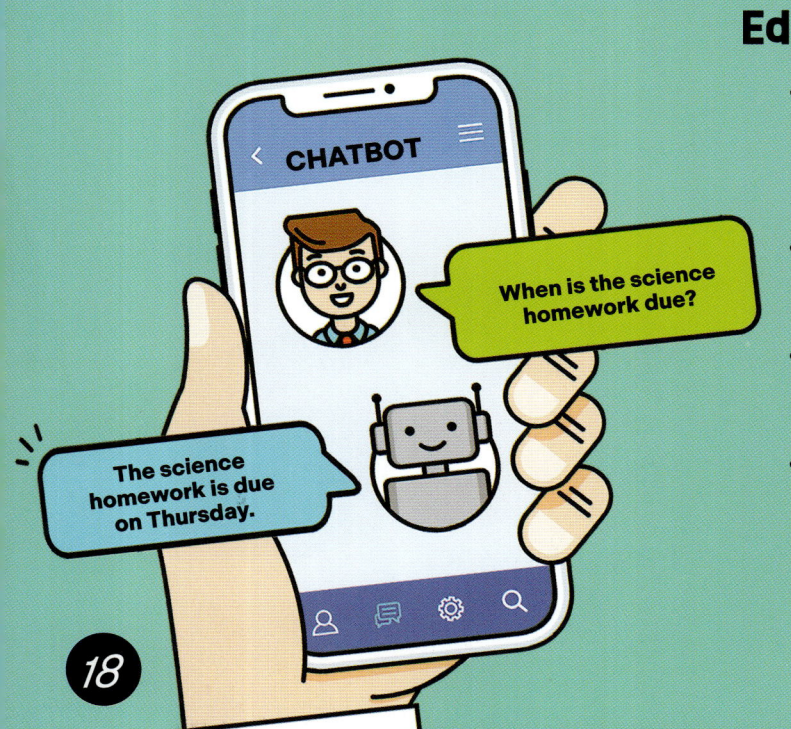

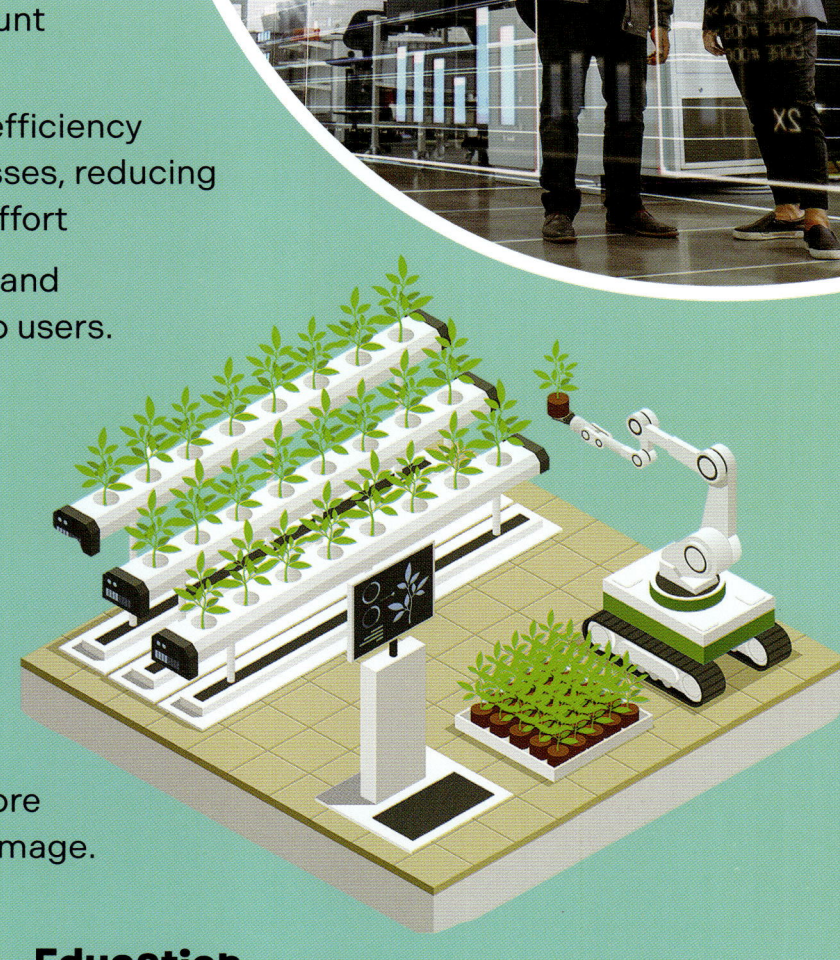

At home

AI is used in smart assistants at home that can recognise spoken instructions, answer questions, complete tasks and control other devices (*more on how these work on pages 26–27*).

We also have automatic cleaning devices! Some self-powered vacuum cleaners and lawn mowers use AI to know where they are, where they should go and what they should avoid.

No cord! No human effort!

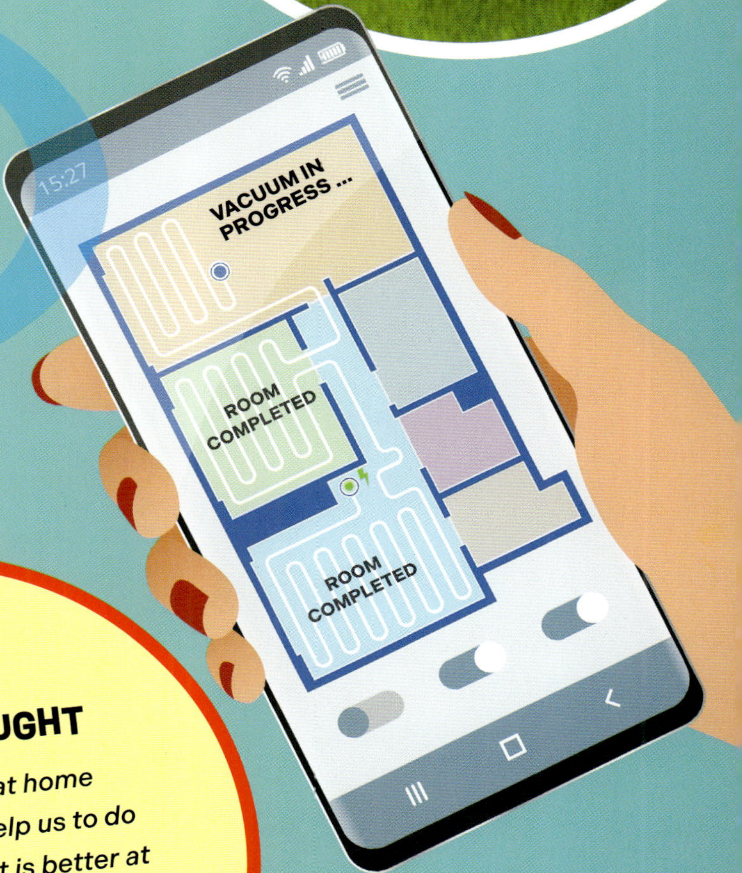

PAUSE FOR THOUGHT

AI can make our lives at home and at work easier and help us to do things better and faster. It is better at some of the tasks that we might struggle with. However, AI is not yet at a stage where we can leave all important decisions to it without doing careful checks.

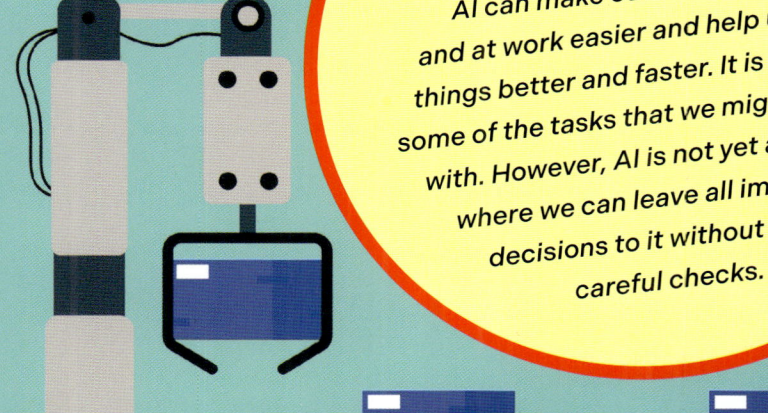

19

Search: AI problem-solving

Some problems have clear solutions and programmers can write instructions to find them. Other times, there are many solutions to a problem, or many possible options in finding a solution. **Search** is an AI technique that can help to choose the best way to solve complex problems.

The problem-solving journey

We can think about solving problems in terms of going from a **starting point** to a **final point**, where the solution is. There may be many points in between that we pass through to get there. In Computer Science and AI, each of these points is called a **state**.

START → S1 (2)
S1 → S2 (3)
S2 → FINISH (5)
S1 → S3 (1) [from S3 to S1]
S2 → S4 (3)
START → S3 (3)
S3 → S4 (4)
S4 → S5 (2)
S5 → FINISH (2)
S3 → S5 (8)

The **states** in a problem

states — cost of each step

Search: the solution

Search algorithms in AI help find a route from the starting state to the final state. They decide which states along the way should be chosen next. For example, search is used in games, such as chess and Tic-Tac-Toe, to decide how to make moves.

Going from one state to another usually has a cost (time, effort or resources). Ideally, we want our search to find a route with the **least cost**, to solve the problem efficiently.

20

Where are search methods used?

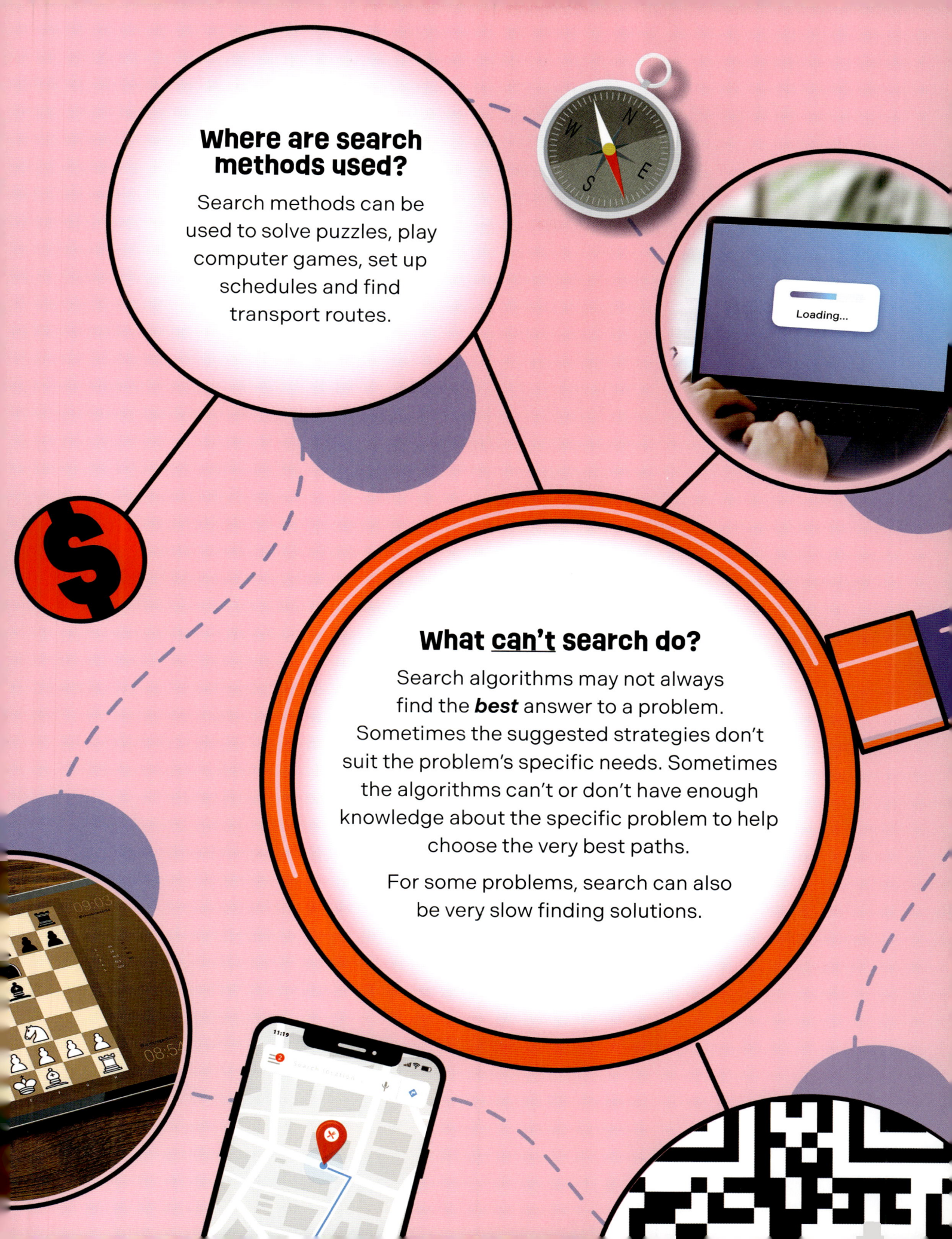

Search methods can be used to solve puzzles, play computer games, set up schedules and find transport routes.

What can't search do?

Search algorithms may not always find the ***best*** answer to a problem. Sometimes the suggested strategies don't suit the problem's specific needs. Sometimes the algorithms can't or don't have enough knowledge about the specific problem to help choose the very best paths.

For some problems, search can also be very slow finding solutions.

Example 1: Game engines

AI has had a huge impact on video games. It has allowed more complex and interesting games to be created.

The engine behind the game

A *game engine* is a computer program that developers use to make video games. It can speed up game development and testing.

What parts do game engines have?

- *Input*: turns actions from players into events within the game.
- *Physics engine*: produces realistic movements in the game, based on real-world laws of physics.
- *Graphics engine*: produces a 2- or 3-D image from models.
- *Logic and AI*: improves the game's behaviour and helps other parts of the engine run smoothly.
- *Sound engine*: manages sound effects.
- *Networking*: allows gameplay with others in different locations using the internet.

How is AI used in game engines?

AI improves the gaming experience in many ways, for example, by:

- producing realistic effects for characters and scenes, based on real-world data
- generating game content quickly, such as levels, maps, landscapes and missions
- providing hints and recommendations for next moves in real time for users
- making intelligent virtual characters for users to interact with.

What AI methods are used in gaming?

Search (*see pages 20–21*) is used for game-playing AI to plan moves.

Machine learning (*see pages 32–33*) is used to generate content and learn players' preferences as they play.

Natural language processing (*see pages 24–25*) is used for interacting with human players and for creating game storylines.

Natural language processing

Natural language processing (NLP) is the ability of computer programs to understand written or spoken human language. It uses ideas from both linguistics (the study of language) and computer science, particularly AI.

What can NLP programs do?

These interactive programs can:

- **respond** to spoken commands in natural language
- **translate** from one language to another
- **sum up** large amounts of information in simple, natural language.

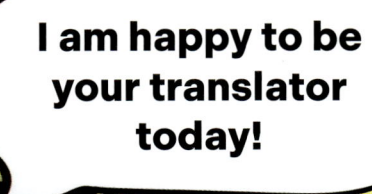

I am happy to be your translator today!

How do NLP programs do it?

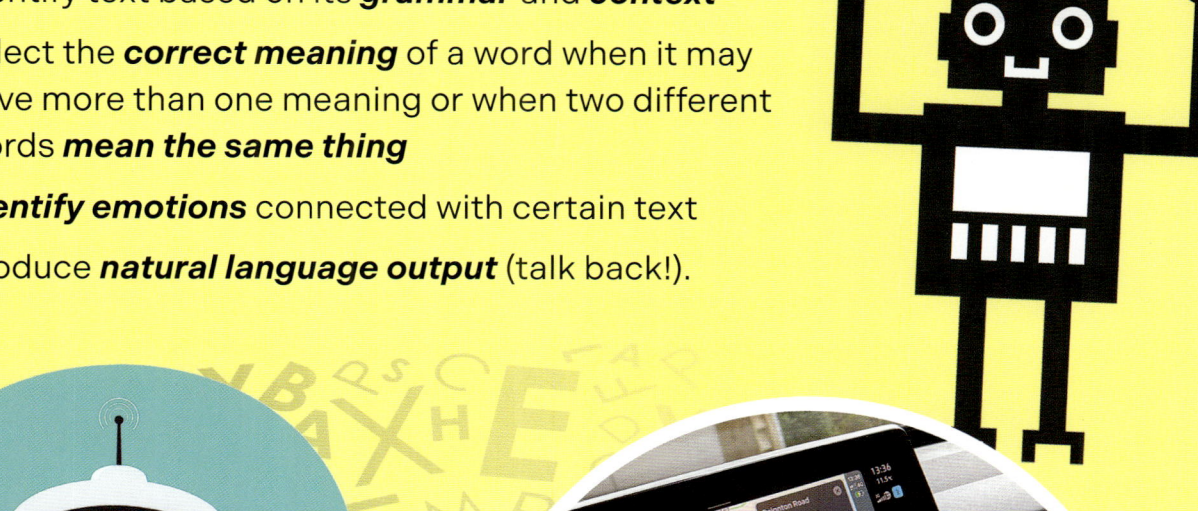

In order to function in their key roles for humans, NLP programs need to be able to:

- recognise **voice data** (humans speaking) and turn that into **text data** to analyse
- identify text based on its **grammar** and **context**
- select the **correct meaning** of a word when it may have more than one meaning or when two different words **mean the same thing**
- **identify emotions** connected with certain text
- produce **natural language output** (talk back!).

Where is NLP used?

NLP is used in applications such as:

- *smart assistants*
- *satnav systems*
- *dictation software (speech to text or the other way around)*
- *customer service chatbots*
- *language translation software.*

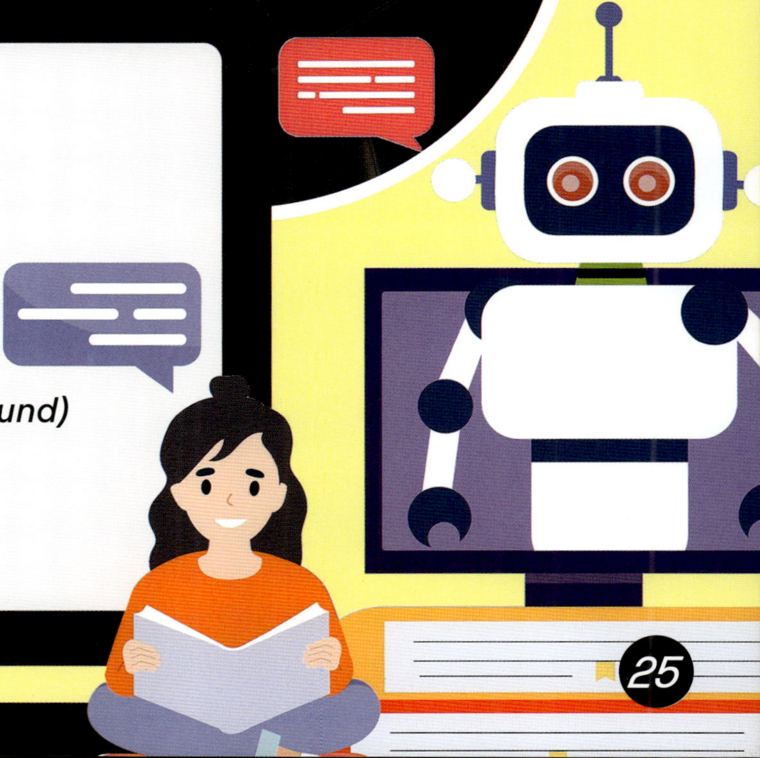

25

Example 2: Smart assistants

Smart assistants are programs that can complete tasks based on voice commands from users. They are included in many devices, such as smartphones, tablets, laptops and smart speakers.

What can a smart assistant do?

When given voice commands, smart assistants can do many tasks for their human users, such as:

- find information, for example, the weather forecast
- control devices or apps to, for example, turn on lights or music
- make phone calls or send texts
- update diaries and set reminders
- order shopping and make bookings using online services.

Some smart assistants will also accept text commands if speech is not an option.

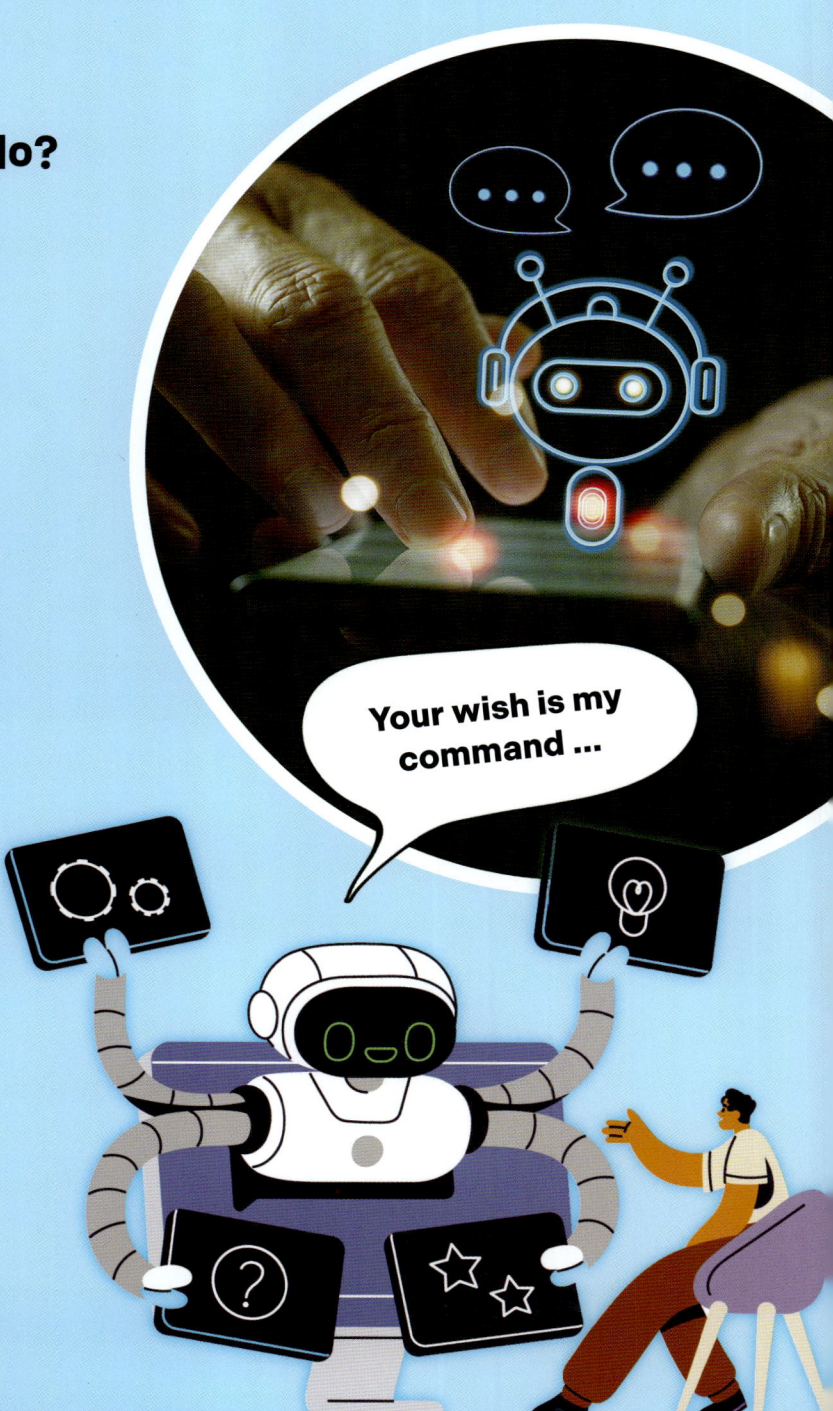

Your wish is my command ...

Which AI methods are used to make smart assistants?

- **Natural language processing** is used when listening for spoken commands or producing responses.
- **Image recognition** is used when recognising people or digital images.
- **Machine learning** is used to learn user preferences and habits.

PAUSE FOR THOUGHT

Smart assistants can save time and effort for people. They are also very useful for people with certain disabilities, since they are voice-activated and do not need physical activation.

However, there are concerns regarding privacy (they are always listening!) and chances of mistakes when using their services.

I can hear you all the time ...

Robotics

Robotics combines engineering and computer science to build machines (robots) that can do tasks with little need for human intervention.

What can these robots do for us?

Each robot is programmed to do a specific task. Usually, tasks performed by robots are either **too difficult** for humans, require **more strength** than humans have or are **very repetitive**.

An AI boost

Roboticists – who design, build or program robots – don't **have** to use AI, but they are using it more and more to improve their robots' performance, accuracy and usability.

An engineer programs a robotic arm in a 'smart factory' to do a particular job.

What parts make up a robot?

- **a power supply,** to provide energy
- **sensors,** to collect information about the environment in which the robot operates
- **a controller,** to act as the 'brain' of the robot, processing information and making decisions
- **effectors,** which allow the robot to change its environment (do its work)
- **actuators,** which allow the robots to operate (use) its effectors.

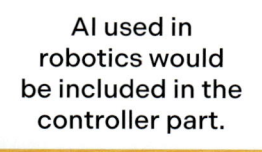

AI used in robotics would be included in the controller part.

What AI methods are used in robots?

- **Computer vision** (AI that allows computers to analyse and understand digital images) is used in 'seeing' their environment.
- **Machine learning** (*see pages 32–33*) is used in recognising objects and making decisions on what to do next.
- **Natural language processing** (*see pages 24–25*) is used in understanding voice commands.

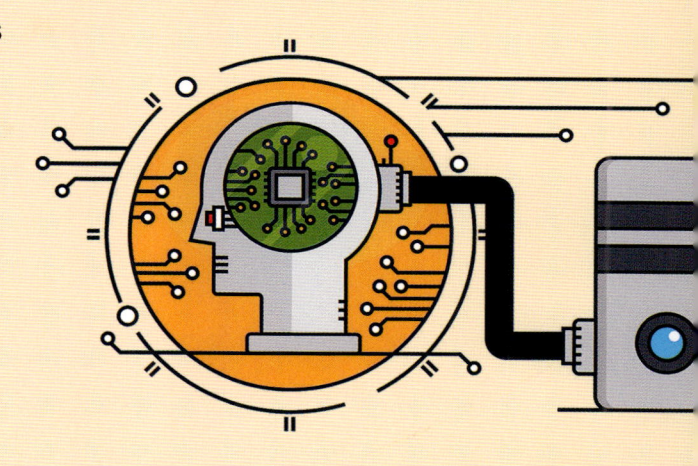

Where can I find robots?

Robots are used in some fascinating places, including:

- assembly lines in factories, building anything from cars to other robots!
- as household devices, such as vacuum cleaners and lawn mowers
- harvesting produce and watering plants on farms
- helping with surgeries and tests in healthcare
- helping with missions to explore harsh environments that humans can't.

Example 3: Autonomous cars

An autonomous car can operate without a human driver. It can sense its surroundings and make decisions based on what it encounters.

What levels of automation are there in cars?

There can be six levels of automation in cars, from level 0 to level 5.

0 — NO AUTOMATION
The driver has full control of the driving tasks.

1 — DRIVER ASSISTANCE
The vehicle features a single automated system.

2 — PARTIAL AUTOMATION
The vehicle can perform steering and acceleration.

3 — CONDITIONAL AUTOMATION
The vehicle can control most driving tasks.

4 — HIGH AUTOMATION
The vehicle performs all driving tasks under certain conditions.

5 — FULL AUTOMATION
The vehicle performs all driving tasks under all conditions.

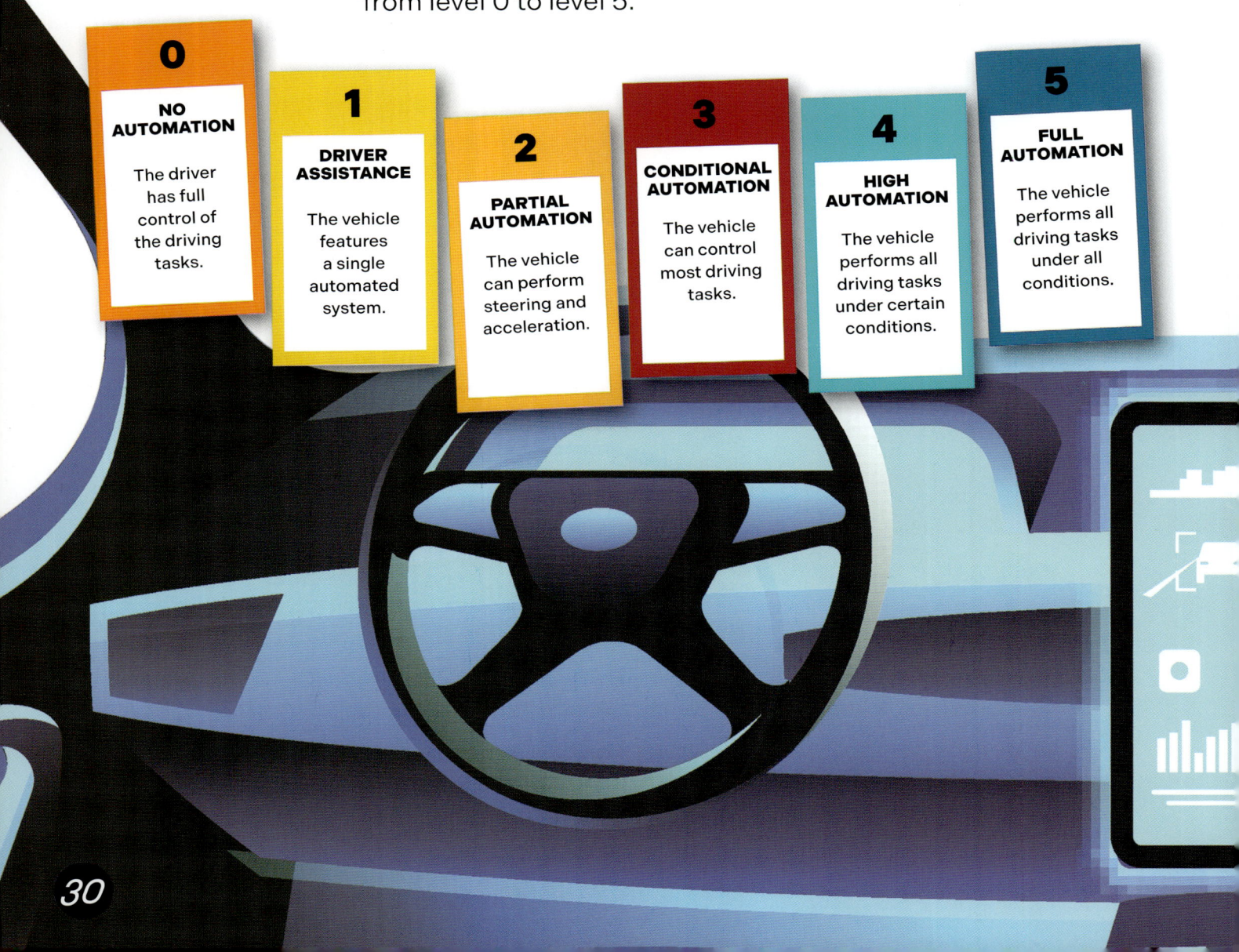

How do autonomous cars work?

Sensors placed around the car can 'see' vehicles and pedestrians nearby, read traffic lights and road signs, understand road markings and measure distances.

The **complex software** run by **powerful computers** uses this information to set a safe route to the destination.

Instructions are sent to the **actuators** to control the car's movement (*as in robots, see pages 28–29*).

What AI methods are in use?

AI in these vehicles includes *computer vision* and *machine learning*:

- recognising obstacles and understanding how they might affect the journey
- reading traffic signs
- predicting problems based on the circumstances.

PAUSE FOR THOUGHT

As with anything fully automated, there are concerns as well as benefits with autonomous cars.

*What about a situation where **any** decision the car makes would be bad for at least someone (an ethical dilemma)? How does the software decide what to do?*

Human drivers use more than data about distance, signs and markings to decide what to do. For example, facial expressions of other drivers can make a difference to our choices. AI can't do this well yet.

Machine learning

Machine learning is such a popular idea, it is sometimes confused with **all** of AI.

What is machine learning?

In machine learning, software is able to learn how inputs and outputs are related by **finding patterns** in data, without being given rules. It can then use what it learns to produce outputs for **different** inputs.

Software that uses machine learning has three main parts: an **algorithm**, **data** and a **model**. The algorithm learns the patterns and represents this in the model. We can then use the model to solve **new** problems.

Why do we want machines to learn?

Sometimes we need to create software that can deal with large amounts of data and solve complicated problems. In these cases, it can be very difficult to precisely write down all the rules we will need and when each rule should be used.

Where is machine learning used?

We've seen that machine learning is used as a **part** of other areas of AI. Further uses include:

- **search engines** that learn user behaviour to improve how they rank search results
- **spam filters** that continuously learn about new spamming methods to improve their performance
- **content moderators in social media** that analyse large amounts of content and identify posts that break community rules
- **fraud detectors in banking** that learn about typical user behaviour, so that any unusual activity can be flagged up.

PAUSE FOR THOUGHT

Machine learning can be used to solve many different types of problem. But ...

- We don't always know how the software produces its results, so we can't be sure that the results are always correct.
- The quality of the results depends on the amount and quality of data used to train the software.

Bad data = bad results

- Some machine learning software might do things that are unfair. For example, it can use people's online content without permission or without giving them credit.

Example 4: Generative AI

Generative AI is a form of machine learning. Given a written description, generative AI programs can produce the requested text, music, computer programs, images or video.

How does generative AI work?

Generative AI uses neural networks, computer systems modelled on the human brain, to look for patterns in existing data. It can then use these patterns to **create new content**.

Generative AI uses many different kinds of machine learning for training its models, so that it can learn quickly from large amounts of data.

Draw me a picture of a cactus in the style of Salvador Dalí, please ...

Where can we use generative AI?

- It can be used to make animations, videos, stories and images for near-instant enjoyment.
- It is useful in healthcare to make new biological structures that don't exist in nature yet, so scientists can make new and better medicines quicker.
- And it can be used at work or school to write emails or responses to questions.

PAUSE FOR THOUGHT

For some types of outputs by generative AI, as with machine learning, the quality is hard to guarantee.

Generative AI also tends to need a lot of computing resources to operate. It can be very expensive to develop and maintain.

There are also worries that online content is being used to train generative AI without permission from the creators, and without checks on the content's biases (unfair preferences).

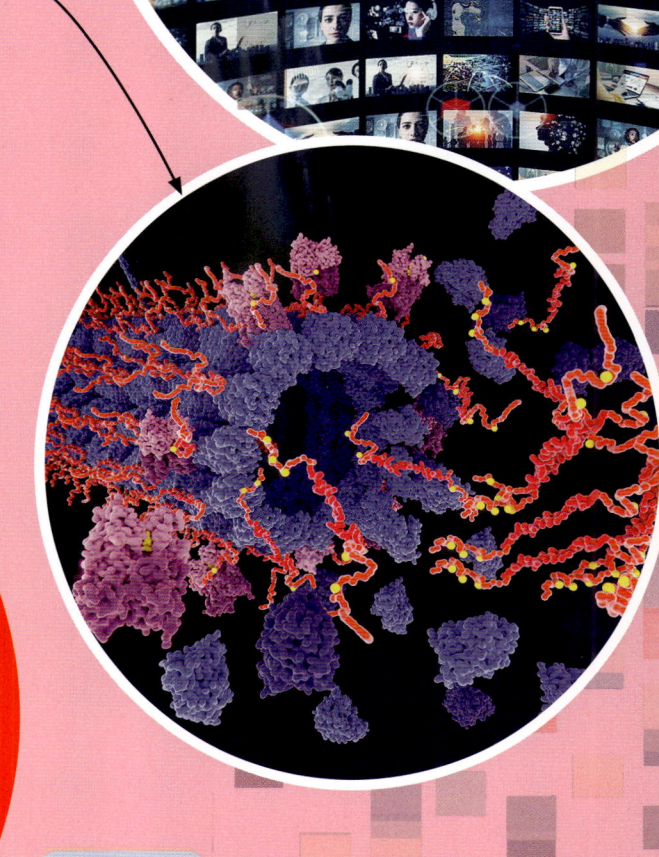

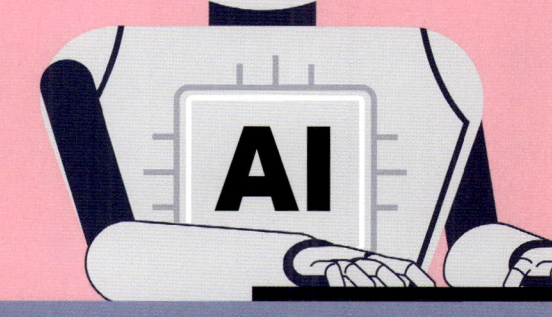

Roses are red,
Violets are blue,
Is this your copyright?
Who knew?!

What should AI do? The rights and wrongs

The benefits of AI can accomplish great things, and its risks can cause serious problems. We must consider the full impact of an AI method before we decide to use it.

What are the possible benefits of AI?

We've seen how AI can help us solve difficult problems, offer new insights, make discoveries and automate tasks that are too difficult or too boring for humans.

By opening up these options for humans, AI can improve our knowledge, and speed up advances in science and healthcare.

The freedom to pass tasks to AI and make jobs more efficient has the potential to benefit the entire world.

What are the concerns about AI?

The uncontrolled use of AI, even for a purpose that seems good, can have results we don't plan.

- AI algorithms making faulty decisions – without users knowing – can lead to unfair outcomes for many people.
- AI trained on biased data can create or continue biases when it is used.
- If we depend on AI too much, humans may lose interest in improving our knowledge and thinking about rights and wrongs of decisions.
- AI programs often need a lot of hardware and computing power to do their work. This energy cost can have a negative impact on our planet.

How do we think about this?

We need to think about what it means to use an AI program, not just for ourselves but for others.

We need to hold on to our responsibility for important decisions when they can affect many people.

Ideally, humans can agree to work towards having 'responsible automation' through AI that can benefit all of us and our planet.

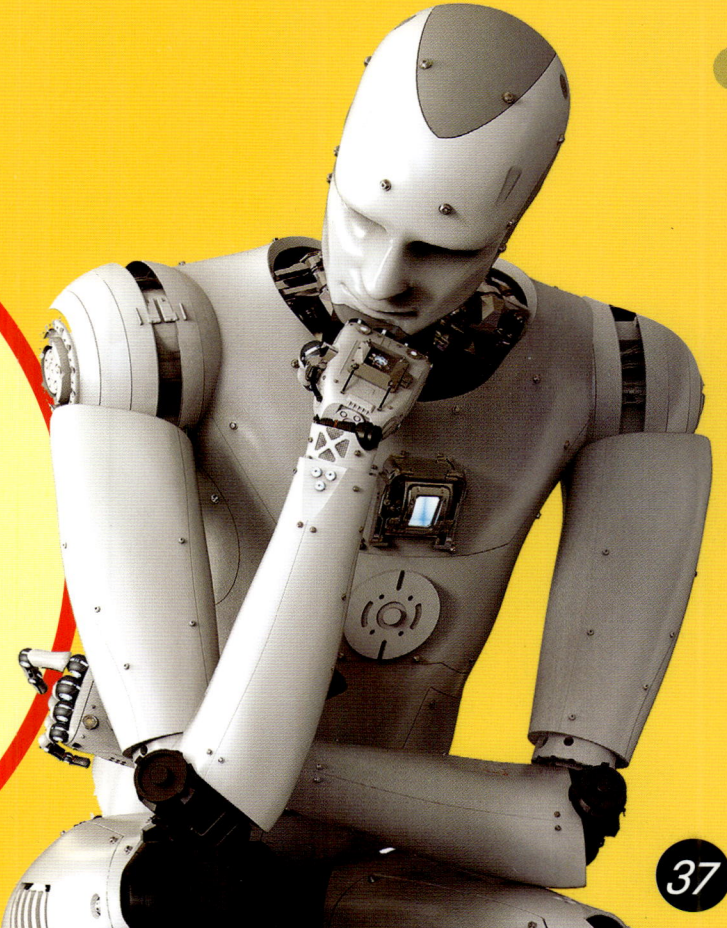

What is the future of AI?

As more work is done on AI in universities and businesses, and as it becomes better known, AI is likely to be used in most parts of our lives. Here are a few areas where AI could make a significant difference in the future.

Doctor AI

AI has the potential to make dramatic progress in preventing illnesses. Scientists are also working towards surgery, diagnoses and treatment fully directed by AI. Imagine being able to call a holographic doctor anytime you want, or having medicines made just for you when you need them!

AI as business

AI is also important for boosting economies around the world. Experts predict that money made from AI software worldwide will be worth over US$125 billion ($125,000,000,000 – that's a lot of zeros!) very soon, and growing quickly each year.

Creative AI

Generative AI can already produce new 'creative' content. In the future, AI is likely to have a bigger impact on creative industries such as fashion, architecture and fine art. We may even have wearable language translators, just as characters do in science fiction!

> How do you think wearable translators could impact language-learning in the future?

Evolution of robots

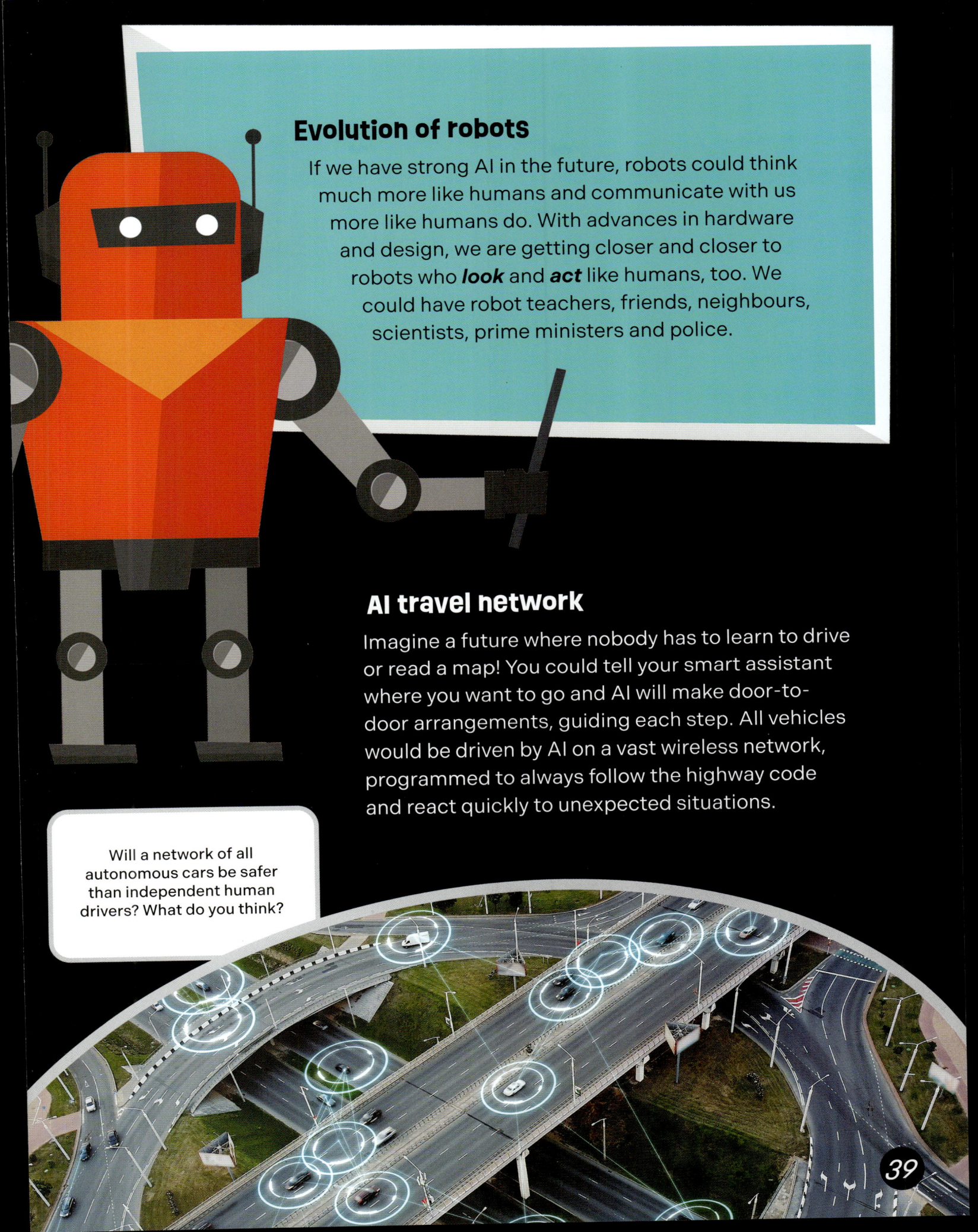

If we have strong AI in the future, robots could think much more like humans and communicate with us more like humans do. With advances in hardware and design, we are getting closer and closer to robots who *look* and *act* like humans, too. We could have robot teachers, friends, neighbours, scientists, prime ministers and police.

AI travel network

Imagine a future where nobody has to learn to drive or read a map! You could tell your smart assistant where you want to go and AI will make door-to-door arrangements, guiding each step. All vehicles would be driven by AI on a vast wireless network, programmed to always follow the highway code and react quickly to unexpected situations.

Will a network of all autonomous cars be safer than independent human drivers? What do you think?

What other subjects are useful for AI?

It's not just computer science! A good grasp of varied subjects is useful for developing and understanding AI well.

Philosophy

Philosophy is the study of the nature of the world and everything in it, including what knowledge *is* and how to tell right from wrong. It is important to AI because it can help us answer questions, such as:

- How should we go from **knowing** something to **acting** on it, in our lives as humans and in our AI practice?
- Is the action we are planning to take **morally right** and how do we know?

Mathematics

Maths is an important foundation for all of computer science, including AI. It can help us answer questions, such as:

- What **rules** can we use to reach **reliable** answers?
- If we are not sure about the data's quality, what kind of decisions **can** we make from analysing the data we have?
- What kind of **complex problems** can we solve with AI?

Psychology

Psychology is a method of studying the mind, brain and how people behave. For AI, psychology can help us answer questions, such as:

- How do humans **think, learn** and **act**?
- How does the **human brain** process information?
- How can we **model** and **improve on** human behaviour in AI? What does improving on it **mean**?

Linguistics

Linguistics is the study of languages, how they are formed and how they change over time. It can help answer questions, such as:

- How can we write programs that can understand human languages **of all kinds**?
- How do we train AI programs to produce **correct** language output, and get better at 'sounding human'?

Statistics

Statistics is the subject related to how we collect, understand and present data. A lot of AI methods learn from data using statistical models. They help us answer questions, such as:

- What useful **patterns** can we find in the data we have?
- What is statistically **likely** to happen in the future, given the data we have?
- How **good** are our AI algorithms?

What if? ???????

What if people rely on AI too much?

We want to use AI in a way that benefits everyone. We know AI can do a lot of good. But it is possible to use it in ways that are not fair to people, or take away their individual freedom or privacy. Even if we don't mean to do this, it might happen because we don't think about it carefully. Overusing AI can affect a few people or lots of people.

We need to be aware of the use of AI in all aspects of our lives so that we can understand its effects.

? ? ? ? ?

Although AI can make our lives easier in many ways, we want to keep thinking, learning and exploring on our own as well, because those are the things that make our lives really interesting.

What if AI takes all our jobs?

Some people might worry that, as AI gets better, it might take their jobs away. More jobs may indeed get automated, but these changes should be done in a way to help the human workers find new ways to use their skills, or new exciting skills to learn.

There will always be jobs that need human judgement, empathy, decisions and creativity. And a more-automated future will have new jobs that don't exist yet!

Of course, increased AI development also means we will need more computer scientists and researchers who understand AI, write good AI programs and help others to use AI properly.

What if AI hurts our planet?

We need to think about the benefits and risks of AI for our planet, too. AI can help us work efficiently, reduce our energy use and increase productivity. It can help us explore difficult problems, such as climate change. All of this will help our planet, too.

However, AI usually needs a lot of resources to operate, and that has an impact on the planet. We need to look for more efficient ways AI can be used. AI might even help us with this AI problem!

How would you like to use AI?

So far, we have looked at what AI is, how it works, some of the things it can do for us and some of the things we need to consider when using AI. Try to imagine how you would like to use AI in the following settings.

At home

At school

In sports

For entertainment

For travel

To keep in touch with family and friends

Glossary

Agriculture: the activity of growing crops (such as wheat or carrots) and livestock (such as chicken or sheep) to produce food or other useful natural items.

Algorithm: a set of instructions or steps to be followed in solving a problem or completing a task.

Application: a computer program produced for a specific purpose.

Artificial intelligence: the ability of computer programs to imitate the way humans make decisions and solve problems.

Automation: the use of machines to complete tasks, minimising or removing human involvement.

Autonomy: the ability something or someone has to make their own decisions without being controlled by others.

Code breaking: the process of finding out the content of a hidden (or coded) message by someone other than the people meant to receive the message.

Computer: a machine that can run instructions (programs) to complete tasks

Computer vision: a field of AI that allows computer programs to understand digital images and videos.

Customer demand: how much a group of people want to have something specific (for example, a product or service).

Data: information we collect and store about things that are of interest in completing tasks or solving problems.

Decision tree: shows the results of a series of related choices in the form of a tree.

Device: a machine produced for a specific purpose.

Diagnosis: the process of finding out the illness a person has, or a problem with something, based on the knowledge we have.

Dilemma: a difficult situation in which we have to make a choice among options that are not good for everyone involved.

Efficiency: the way of doing the most amount of useful work, while using as little time or money or energy as possible.

Ethics: the study of what is right and wrong and guidance on this topic.

Ethnic group: a group of people who share a common language, culture or nationality.

Expert system: a computer program that uses AI methods to behave like a human expert in a subject.

Generation of content: the process of creating text, images, videos, etc. that will be posted online.

Generative AI: the use of AI to produce different types of content, such as text, image, video, audio, etc.

Hologram: a 3-dimensional (3-D) image.

Input: the set of data required by a computer program to carry out a task.

Intelligence: the ability to gain knowledge and skills, and to use them in a logical and sensible way.

Machine learning: a field of AI that uses data and algorithms to learn to make decisions, as humans might learn from examples.

Model: a way of representing a real life thing or situation, but usually without all the details.

Natural language processing: a field of AI that gives computer programs the ability to understand written or spoken human languages.

Neural network: a computer program based on how the human brain works and is a way of realising machine learning.

Output: the data produced as the result of a computer program.

Pioneer: one of the first people to do something.

Productivity: the amount of work a person, a group of people or a company is able to do in a specific amount of time.

Program: a set of instructions written for a computer to carry out.

Robot: a machine that can complete tasks with little or no human involvement.

Routine: a word used to mean a regular or usual way of doing something.

Smart assistant: an AI program that can complete different tasks based on voice commands from users.

Software: a set of programs used for a specific purpose, such as operating a computer or completing some task.

Spam: an unwanted email.

Statistical model: a mathematical model that represents data we have gathered about the real world and allows us to draw conclusions about the data.

Symptom: a physical or mental change that can be caused by an illness.

Virtual: a word used to mean something that does not exist physically, but only digitally.

Further information

More books to read:

A Question of Technology series by Clive Gifford, *Wayland 2023*
- *Who Invented Inventing? And other questions about inventions*
- *Can Light Slice Through Steel? And other questions about machines*
- *What's So Super about Supercomputers? And other questions about computers*
- *Can a Driverless Car Get Lost? And other questions about transport*
- *Can You Break the Internet? And other questions about the Internet*
- *Will Robots Take Over the World? And other questions about AI*
- *Why Do Phone Calls Travel into Space? And other questions about electronics*
- *How Do You Go to Toilet in Space? And other questions about space*

The **Explore AI** series by Sonya Newland, *Wayland 2022*
- *Brainy Computers*
- *Intelligent Robots*
- *Smart Devices*
- *Machine Learning*

Tech-head Guide series by William Potter, *Wayland 2020*
- *Robots*
- *Computers*
- *Drones*
- *AI*

Websites to visit:

Cognimates, an AI education platform for children:
cognimates.me/home/

The AI Challenge from Technovation Families:
www.curiositymachine.org/lessons/lesson/

Interactive machine learning applications to explore with an adult:
magenta.tensorflow.org/demos/web/

The website addresses (URLs) included in this book were valid at the time of going to press. However, it is possible that contents or addresses may have changed since the publication of this book. No responsibility for any such changes can be accepted by either the author or the Publisher.

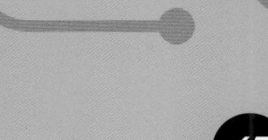

Index

AI pets, *7*
algorithms, *14, 32, 37, 41, 43*
    search algorithms *20–21, 23*
applications/apps, *7, 25, 26, 33*
automation, *14, 19, 30–31, 36, 37, 39, 43*

benefits of A,I *11, 16–19, 36–37, 42–43*
bias in AI learning, *9, 34, 37*
Breazeal, Cynthia, *9*
Buolamwini, Joy, *9*

chatbots, *5, 12, 17, 18, 25*
code breaking, *8*
computer programming, *5, 6, 8, 10, 11, 20, 22, 28, 32, 39*
computer programs, *5, 6, 7, 8, 9, 10, 14, 18, 22–23, 24, 26–27, 34, 37, 41, 43*
computers, *4, 7, 16, 26, 29, 31*
computer vision, *9, 29, 31*
connectionist, AI *14–15*

Dalí, Salvador, *34*
dangers of AI, *9, 19, 27, 31, 33, 35, 36–37, 42–43*
data, *7, 10–13, 14, 15, 16, 17, 18, 23, 25, 31, 32, 33, 34, 36, 37, 40, 41*
decision-making, *4, 5, 8, 10–13, 14, 15, 16–19, 20, 25, 28, 29, 30–31, 37, 38, 39, 40, 45*
deep learning, *9*

education, *9, 18, 35, 36, 39, 44*
engineering, *5, 28*
ethics (of AI), *9, 31, 33, 35, 37, 40*
expert systems, *6, 15*

facial recognition, (see *visual recognition*)
factories, *18, 88, 29*
farming, *18, 29*

game engines, *22–23*
games, *6, 7, 8, 9, 10, 15, 17, 20, 21, 22–23, 45*
    chess, *6, 7, 20, 21, 23*
    video games, *17, 22–23*
generative AI, *7, 22–23, 34–35, 38*
    art, *7, 34, 35, 38*
    stories, *7, 35*
Grosz, Barbara J. *9*

healthcare, *9, 11, 16, 29, 35, 36, 38*
Hinton, Geoffrey, *9*
household devices, *7, 19, 29, 44*

jobs and AI, *11, 14, 28, 36, 37, 38–39, 43*

Kasparov, Gary, *7*

logic, *4, 5, 22*

machine learning, *6, 8, 9, 15, 23, 27, 29, 31, 32–35*
    neural networks *6, 15, 34*
McCarthy, John, *5, 8*
models, *6, 15, 22, 32, 34, 41*

narrow AI, *5*
natural intelligence, *4*
natural language processing, *6, 9, 13, 23, 24–25, 27, 29, 41*

online, *13, 17, 26, 33, 35*

prediction, *11, 13, 18, 31*
privacy, *27, 42*
problem-solving, *5, 9, 10, 11, 13, 14, 15, 18, 19, 20–21, 32, 33, 36, 40, 43*

robotics, *8, 9, 28–29*
robots, *6, 7, 9, 12, 28–29, 31, 39*

Samuel, Arthur, *8*
science, *5, 16, 36*
scientists, *11, 16, 35, 38, 39, 43*
search engines, *33*
Second World War, *8*
self-driving vehicles *7, 8, 39*
    cars *6, 30–31, 39*
sensors, *28, 31*
shopping, *10, 16, 17, 26*
smart assistants, *7, 8, 19, 25, 26–27, 39*
smartphones, *7, 26*
social media, *33*
software, *7, 10, 25, 31, 32, 33, 38*
space, *7, 16, 29*
speech recognition, *7, 8, 9, 13, 19, 24, 25, 26–27, 29*
strong AI, *5, 39*
Suleyman, Mustafa, *9*
symbolic AI, *14–15*

Turing, Alan, *6, 8*
Turing Test, *6, 8*

visual recognition, *9, 13, 27, 31*

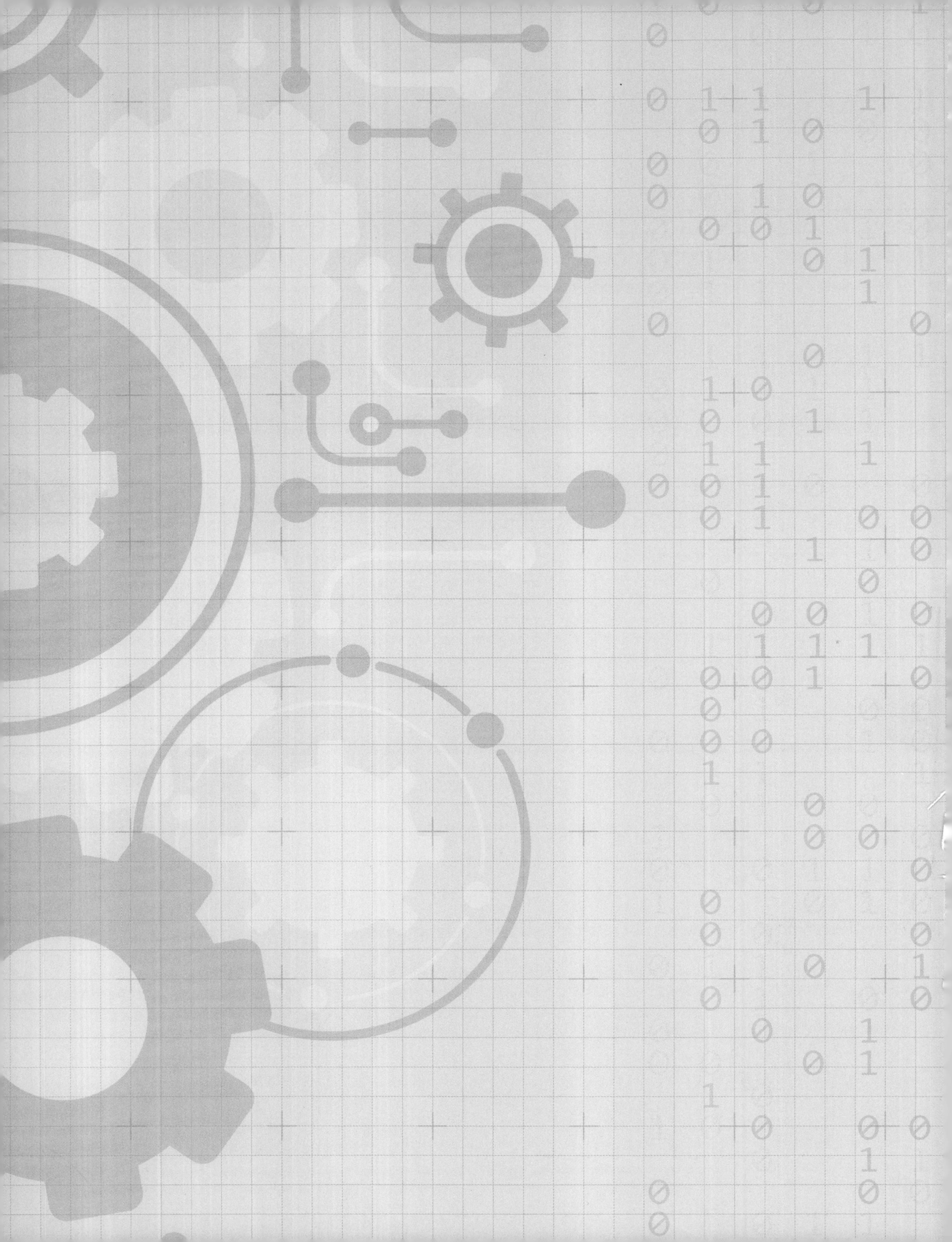